SPORTS BIOGRAPHIES

COOPER KUPP

KENNY ABDO

Fly!
An Imprint of Abdo Zoom
abdobooks.com

abdobooks.com

Published by Abdo Zoom, a division of ABDO, P.O. Box 398166, Minneapolis, Minnesota 55439. Copyright © 2023 by Abdo Consulting Group, Inc. International copyrights reserved in all countries. No part of this book may be reproduced in any form without written permission from the publisher. Fly!™ is a trademark and logo of Abdo Zoom.

Printed in the United States of America, North Mankato, Minnesota.
102022
012023

Photo Credits: Alamy, Getty Images, iStock, Shutterstock
Production Contributors: Kenny Abdo, Jennie Forsberg, Grace Hansen
Design Contributors: Neil Klinepier

Library of Congress Control Number: 2022937321

Publisher's Cataloging-in-Publication Data

Names: Abdo, Kenny, author.
Title: Cooper Kupp / by Kenny Abdo
Description: Minneapolis, Minnesota : Abdo Zoom, 2023 | Series: Sports biographies | Includes online resources and index.
Identifiers: ISBN 9781098280239 (lib. bdg.) | ISBN 9781098280765 (ebook) | ISBN 9781098281069 (Read-to-Me ebook)
Subjects: LCSH: Wide receivers (Football)--Juvenile literature. | Rams (Football team)--Juvenile literature. | American football--Juvenile literature. | Professional athletes--Biography--Juvenile literature.
Classification: DDC 796.092--dc23

TABLE OF CONTENTS

Cooper Kupp 4

Early Years 8

Going Pro 12

Legacy 18

Glossary 22

Online Resources 23

Index 24

COOPER KUPP

In his young career, Cooper Kupp has already received enough attention to become an NFL fan favorite.

After setting many records and securing a **Super Bowl** ring, Kupp has earned the title of the best wide receiver in the game today.

EARLY YEARS

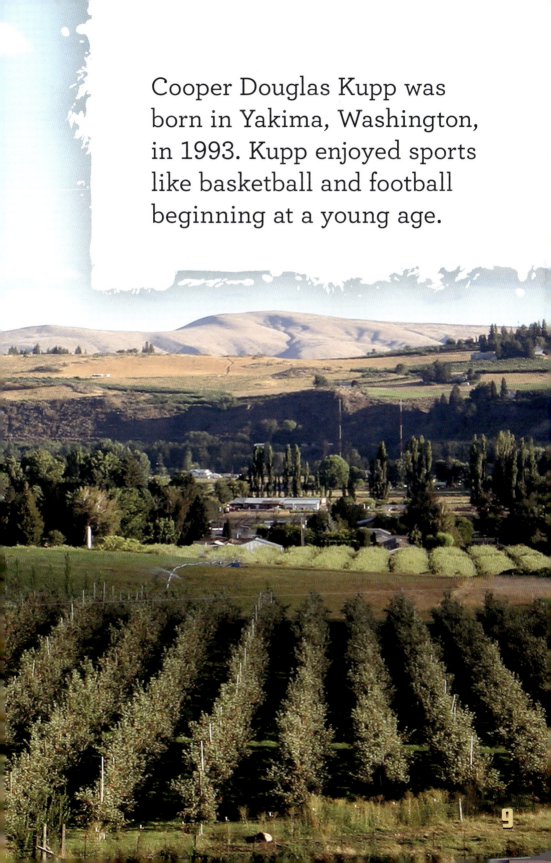

Cooper Douglas Kupp was born in Yakima, Washington, in 1993. Kupp enjoyed sports like basketball and football beginning at a young age.

Professional football runs throughout Kupp's family. His dad, Craig, was a quarterback for the Cardinals and the Cowboys. His grandfather, Jake, was a guard for many teams.

Kupp attended college at Eastern Washington University. He led his team to the **playoffs** three out of four years. Kupp was also the college football all-division career leader in receiving yards with 6,464.

GOING PRO

The Los Angeles Rams **drafted** Kupp in 2017. The team won the **NFC** West division that season! Kupp was added to the All-**Rookie** Team by the Pro Football Writers Association.

Partway through the 2018 season, Kupp tore his **ACL**. The Rams still made it to **Super Bowl** LIII. Unfortunately, they lost 13–3 to the New England Patriots.

Kupp was back on the field for the 2019 season. During the NFL London Games, he set a record for most receiving yards in an international game.

For the 2020 season, Kupp swapped his number 18 jersey for 10. It was the number he wore in college. But Kupp was **sidelined** once again after hurting his knee before the **playoffs**.

In 2021, Kupp secured a rare **triple crown** season. At **Super Bowl** LVI, he made the game-winning touchdown against the Bengals. Kupp was named the **MVP** of the game.

LEGACY

Kupp is a very active volunteer with many charities. He has worked with organizations like Second Harvest, which helps fight hunger throughout America.

Kupp is one of two players named AP Offensive Player of the Year and **Super Bowl MVP** in the same season. With that kind of start, there is no telling how far his career will go.

GLOSSARY

anterior cruciate ligament (ACL) – one of the four main muscles that stabilizes the knee joint.

draft – a process in sports to assign athletes to a certain team.

MVP – short for "most valuable player," an award given in sports to a player who has performed the best in a game or series.

National Football Conference (NFC) – one of two major conferences of the NFL. The winner of the NFC championship plays the AFC winner at the Super Bowl.

playoffs – a single-elimination tournament held after the regular season to determine the NFL champion.

rookie – a first-year player in a professional sport.

sidelined – an athlete who is prevented from playing or competing and can only watch.

Super Bowl – the NFL championship game, played once a year.

triple crown – when a player is the leader in receptions, receiving yards, and receiving touchdowns in a season.

ONLINE RESOURCES

To learn more about Cooper Kupp, please visit **abdobooklinks.com** or scan this QR code. These links are routinely monitored and updated to provide the most current information available.

INDEX

Cardinals (team) 10

charity work 18

Cowboys (team) 10

Eastern Washington University 11, 16

family 10

injuries 14, 16

Patriots (team) 14

Rams (team) 12

records 11, 15, 17, 20

Super Bowl 14, 17, 20

Washington 9